Ada Prisco

A night

Youcanprint *Self-Publishing*

Titolo | A night
Autore | Ada Prisco

Immagine di copertina a cura dell'autrice

ISBN | 978-13-26776-12-1

Youcanprint Self-Publishing
Via Roma, 73 - 73039 Tricase (LE) - Italy
www.youcanprint.it
info@youcanprint.it
Facebook: facebook.com/youcanprint.it
Twitter: twitter.com/youcanprintit

To Hosam Amer
met
that night

A NIGHT

Preface

This little book of poetries without rhymes and with no pretensions is like a travel started from a single moment, almost quietly; it was born during a spring night very very late, at the time when a tired day leaves and another one is raising shyly, in the darkness that doesn't dare to say not the dawn that is coming.

Like every book, and especially like every poetic book, it is not a diary, it doesn't show a report. The real event has been described and explained in the light of fantasy and feelings. Above all the night of the title has been seen here as a source of inspiration.

Besides the true and direct experience, the meaning of the night can become a symbol and it can be valid for anyone. It's the unexpected chance that happens and, whatever you are doing or you are planning, changes your life. It's also something completely new and unknown. Sure, the danger is the fear. The fear closes, the trust opens.

This book wouldn't exist if the fear had determined the situation. Night is a blind leap. And the day that follows is not the distance from the point you jump and that one you land, because they can be near apparently or equal to your usual life. The night means something if something was born from that, if it shows something you never saw before, an unexplored quality of life, a bigger capability of love.

It's the first time I wrote directly in a language different from mine. It's not because I know English so well! It shares the change I talked about. I left here my native language to get someone else and to be able to express myself and be understood.

It is a symbol too. To get others we have to translate ourselves, to make us understandable. I think this work doesn't finish with the language, it concerns every day, as every day you had to say: "I have to try to understand and to let me understand because he, or she, is important for me, I want to get him, or her". If always we did this exercise, if whole people in the world did the same, the level of peace and harmony would be more and more higher. The night is a gym and you train to meet the other.

The other and the meeting with him or her is the real day that each of us waits, the symbolical night offers the opportunity only. You drawn the picture, the night is the frame.

I.

Angel driver

Remember to welcome strangers
In your homes.
There were some
Who did that
And welcomed angels without knowing it (He 13,2).

In a night as so many others,
In a time as any other,
A stranger taxi driver
Welcomed me as a familiar one.
He wasn't a taxi driver,
He took me away from the danger.
Without knowing it,
I called a taxi driver,
I met my angel driver.

II.

I wish

At the beginning of our meeting,
words similar to many others …
what is your name?
which is your dream?

I' m here,
But I'm preparing there.
I followed the trajectory
Of your glaze,
your wish to be better, to be far.
You guessed me in your thinking
And I admired you,
The way you had did,
The study you was doing,
The dream which you were giving shape to.
I felt as I was inside your dream.
With you I saw a world
Waiting for dreams,
Ours too.

III.

Pyramids

Where are you from?
Are you from here?
No, I'm from Egypt,
From Alexandria.

In this way I began to find
A file of yours,
The cord that ties you to the land,
The angels too have an umbilical cord!
Then you told me:
I remember the first time
I went with my school
To visit the pyramids.
I asked myself:
"How did they do to build them?"
I stayed so much time there,
Fixed in front of them.
In that precise moment I saw in you
The same wonderfulness of that
fourteen years old little boy.
And we were there,
In your taxi,
But also in face of the pyramids,
together.
I felt as I were your eyes.

IV.

A little of sun

I was turn off,
You took a little of
Your land's sun
And you put it
Inside me.

V.

It's a shame

You didn't leave me,
I cannot, you said,
You didn't leave me,
How do you stay here alone?
You didn't leave me,
In my country, in Italy too
Leaving a women on the road
It's a shame, you said,
You didn't leave me,
I'll still stay ten minutes with you,
You didn't leave me.
From then you didn't leave me,
You are inside me,
With me.
Leaving is a shame,
You didn't leave me.

VI.

In heaven

Don't thank me, you said,
It's normal,
Then you added
It should be normal.
Maybe you're right,
It's normal,
But where?
It's normal in heaven
And, in that moment,
I was there,
With you.

VII.

I'm a muslim

What will you do here? You asked.
I knew,
It was dangerous,
I answered: *I'll commend myself to God.*
Talking about God
In a taxi,
A thing that I never did before.

Are you a believer?
You said: *I'm a muslim,*
All of us are equal in face of Him.
We were two,
But embraced
By big arms,
In big hands,
In the biggest love
Of God
Who created us.
And I said you:
Now you are for me
The evidence that
God exists.
And you still are,
By you God's love arrived till me.

VIII.

Arabic, Italian, English and German

Language and meaning,
Two connected elements
But not always together.
We understood each other.
Which words do you know in Arabic?
And I began:
Qu'rān, shahāda
Salāt, salām,
Hijra, hajj,
Zakāt, sadaqa
From these words
To your world.
And you explained,
But do you know
The meaning?
I do.
But I listened to you another one,
The sense of words
For life.

IX.

Don't be afraid

Many times in the Gospel
Jesus invites:
"don't be afraid".
You said me that night,
Don't be afraid.
I wasn't at all,
Because you were there
With me
Nothing touched me,
If not trust
In you
And you were there
With me.

X.

God's gift

God gave me a gift,
I'm able to help the others.

Wisdom occupies
Your consciousness.
I believe in it:
God gave you this gift
And God gave me You
as a special gift
That night,
A wonderful,
Rare,
Very precious
Gift,
Without I noticed,
Without you noticed.
In a terrible night
I was receiving
The most beautiful gift:
You,
From that night like many others,
You are
In my soul.

Black eyes

What's your eyes' color?
They're colored
By the force of life,
A brown river
Past by the lamp of light,
Brave black eyes
Who smile.

XII.

Cinderella at the airport

In a life something happens
Time by time
And it carries away,
It shakes,
It can be the death, an incident,
a good chance, a deep love.
I was swept away
By a fairy tale.
At an Austrian airport,
In a night,
I became Cinderella
And immediately after a princess.
Who did the magic?
My pumpkin was a big heart
And this became a coach.
Attention, Cinderella!
At midnight the coach
Comes back to be a pumpkin!
Go out! Come back home!
Oh no, I'm already at home, thank you.
I'm still in the pumpkin.

<h1 style="text-align:center">XIII.</h1>

Taking care

Everywhere you can
take care,
If you look at this tree,
If you think of the environment.
Everything requires your care.

Everything is waiting for attention,
It's like water for a flower,
Like thread for an acrobat,
Like breath for a survival,
Like sense for a life.

XIV.

Foolish happiness

A dream night
Is in the dream only,
there's no reason to understand,
neither to say lies.
A dream is true in itself,
till it lasts,
till it holds,
till it's night.

Being alive

What does it mean
Being alive?
Maybe is like waking up
From a long and heavy sleep,
Feeling again the life
That flows like a river inside you,
Turning on the light
In the darkness,
Passing from being one to being two.

XVI.

Stage trick

I had to go,
I was in a hurry,
I thought I had to leave.
And then?
Then, like Jews say at Purim,
Stage trick,
By an unexpected turn of events,
Someone else decided:
"it's time to stop".
But why?
He said: *all has been planned.*
God planned.
Years go on with their flow,
But it can be a moment,
Just a single moment
When everything changes,
As the Purim top.
I don't know anything but that,
I stopped.
If there's a plan,
I'm inside.

XVII.

Others' weight

A big heart,
Able to welcome everyone
Becomes a good,
a precious shelter.
Doing good works is a
Charge of life,
But it's also a charge
on your back.

Be ever light your hearth,
Be ever tender,
Be ever itself.

XVIII.

From … to

You have changed my sadness
Into a joyful dance;
You have taken away my sorrow
And surrounded me with joy (Ps 30,11).

You changed death
Into life,
Distance
Into closeness,
Loneliness
Into communion,
Hurry
Into stop,
Insensitivity
Into sharing,
Two footprints
Into four.

In the darkness

In a darkness
Of a night
A bubble has been shaped
Suspended in time, in space,
In its core
There was light,
Anything else existed,
Only the bubble,
A bubble of light
In the darkness of the night.

XX.

Children

Have you children?
Children are the most important thing.

Who loves children
He grows up the seeds
To collect a day the fruits.
He offers
water
To the thirsty land,
Bread
To the little birds,
Milk
To the little lambs.
He takes on his back
And he walks,
Walks,
Walks….
And he prepares a garden
Called *future*.

XXI.

Trust

To trust
Or not to trust
This is the problem!

Wait for me,
I'll come back
for you.

Will you come back
For me?

Why?
Someone said:
How could you trust him?

Trust past trough a glaze.

Yes, I trusted.
If I didn't, I'd have lost
The special gift
You gave me,
thanks,
God.

XXII.

Time

In my mind
That spring night
The only time I had
Was that one
Of my departure.
Forced to stop
I saw the time
Widening more and more,
Till holding
That I believed I lost,
Time,
But it had another quality,
It was offered,
It was warm,
It was the time
That brings with itself
Life,
Like the blood
Runs toward the limbs
And it keeps them alive.

XXIII.

Wings

Every angel has his wings,
Mine is training,
For now he has only
A car.
His wings are inside,
In his dreams,
In his deep dedication.
If you see a feather
On the road,
Please give it back him,
For sure he'll use it
To write another page
Of project,
Because he isn't able
To stop,
He sits
and immediately after
he stands up,
just like him
his brain works and works again.
He doesn't know,
But he has an angel brain.
What does it mean?
A brain provided with hearth.
Someday he'll notice again.

XXIV.

Home

It lasted less than a second,
It past as a flash
In my mind,
It was a question,
But I tried to keep it away.
I'm coming back home.
Are you sure?
Do you want
to come back home?
In the silence
Of that night
My consciousness
Suggested a strange answer,
No, I don't,
Because here
I'm at home.
But what am I thinking?!
It lasted less than a second,
But it was a voice
From my soul.

XXV.

Frames

In the last instants,
When everything
Maybe will come back
In consciousness,
With all endless emptiness
And the bitter cold,
I'll bring with me
The frames of that night
And its hope
That it could last much longer.

XXVI.

Cherry blossoms

For a littlest
we were in Japan,
where
Students and teachers
Go out from school
Sit and eat together
Under the cherry tree
in the season of its blossoms.

Can it flourish during a night?

Over there they know
That cherry blossoms
Live a shortest life
but during this time
its show is unique.
Sitting at the feet
of a heart cherry tree
a deep, beautiful, light experience,
tomorrow it will be different,
you will be different,
but in just one time
cherry tree offered
all its beauty
for us.

XXVII.

Time and meaning

Time is like
An opened land
In face of you,
Under and around you,
The plants that
Everyone seeds
Are the meaning
linked to that time.

Has maybe a sense
What happens
Day by day?

Everyone looks for
His meaning
And so he goes on
To cultivate his life.

Meanings that don't meet
Each other
Are like dead wood
Intended to be cut away.
When two meanings meet each other
An original plants
Starts to grow up
To give its fruits
In good time.

XXVIII.

Leaving and Keeping

Strong or not,
Beautiful or not,
Deep or not,
Every time rules away.
Chinese people say:
You don't get wet
Twice in the same river.
But always your mind
Is there,
Your heart
Is there,
Your memory
With them.
So what do you leave?
What do you keep?
That night I said:
Thank you.
That night elapsed
It accomplished itself.
That kind gesture
went too.
Now I say
thank you
for something else,
for that I kept with me from then.
I welcomed someone
In my soul

And that event,
Happened that night,
Changed all.
It changed all, yes.
That night became
a wonderful source,
also source of inspiration.

What it still springs
Is totally new,
Is full of life,
it belongs to
the day that
follows the night.

XXIX.

Crumbles of light

Tom Thumb marked his way
With crumbles of bread
To come back home
And birds eat his way.
Like him
I had a little bag
And in that night
Time after time
I saved crumbles,
I collected
One by one
And I keep it
With me.
Of light.
Then I marked my way
With them,
Bright signals
At the sides of the road,
Landmark
When there's fog,
When it's dark,
Reserve of light.
Nobody can
Take them from me,
My crumbles of light.

XXX.

What, Who, Where, When, Why

In my mind
Many times
After that night I asked myself:

What, what happened precisely?
A case as many others?
A case as just oneself?
What, what happened?

Who begun?
Did I choose him?
Because I didn't call the other one,
Because I trusted him,
Because I waited him?
Did he choose me?
He was far,
He introduced himself,
He came.

Where,
Where did I notice
He was special,
At the airport?
In the car?
At the bus stop?
When,
When I cross his glaze

The first time,
When I listened
To his voice
At the first time?
There? After?
Why? Is there a why?
An answer is not,
Questions are,
But, at the end,
They don't matter.
That night matters.

XXXI.

Interlude

Sit next,
Be close,
Stay together,
An interlude
Over great distances.

XXXII.

How much is it worth?

A night,
An hour and a half
in a night,
how much is it worth?

How long
Will it take
To be born?

How long will it take
to die?

I touched the time then,
I noted that
The time has a body too.
And I saw:
Just an hour
Can be as valid as
A whole life.

A thousand years ...
Are like one day;
They are like yesterday,
Already gone,
Like a short hour
In the night (Ps 90, 4).

XXXIII.

Gifts

The rooms of houses,
Our memory,
Our space is full
Of gifts:
for birth,
For birthdays,
for Christmas,
for wedding's day.
Objects,
Signs,
Evidences of special moments.

We never think about
The most important gift,
Time
We give others,
Time
We receive from others.
It hasn't a matter
But it's the only one
That builds human beings.
We are what we are
Also for the whole time
Received from someone
Like a gift,
A gift that can build.

XXXIV.

Baby flower

Like a baby flower
To protect from the cold,
Like a baby flower
To protect from the wind,
Like a baby flower
To protect from the sun,
Like a baby flower
To protect from envy,
Like a little flower
To protect from arrogance,
Like a little flower
To protect from anxiety for tomorrow,
Like a little flower
To protect from distrust,
Like a little flower
To protect with tenderness
And to let it be.

XXXV.

Stars were close

When the night comes
All is in the full darkness,
Stars are your partners
And they look like
More and more close.
You wish you keep them,
You think to enjoy
All their light.
That night
It was like
A wire started
From stars' tips
And It arrived till us.
This wire was the rope
Of a seesaw
That cradled us,
While stars
Were close.

XXXVI.

I'll be here again

Déja vu concerns
our past and present:
you live something
and you feel yourself
in the same situation
for the second time,
like if you had already lived it.
I had not a déjà vu, no.
I took an hour
Perhaps
To understand
Just like a flash,
A déjà vu for the future,
A foreseen,
I was still not gone away
But already I thought
To go back.
I felt:
I'll come back,
But the next time
It will be
for you.

XXXVII.

Writing

Not being able to sleep,
Not being able to think,
Not being able
        To resume life,
        As it was before,
Changing of pace.

Writing was born
From a need,
This need is like a fever,
Writing is a medicine.

Writing is also like a shell:
Who approaches the ear
Can hear the motion
And the scent of the ocean
And he can ride the waves
The waves of that night.

XXXVIII.

Candles and lanterns

Night is strange,
Its darkness
Makes bright
Every gleam.
Night is dangerous,
Night can feed
Poor eyesight.
Every nightly light
Enjoys a giant halo,
For the short-sighted view
Especially.
The tip of the tail
of a tiny firefly
may seem
like the morning star,
it's small,
but it turns on a warning light
in the murk.
By night
It's more easy
Mistaking candles
For lanterns.

XXXIX.

A night, a life, a path

Any nights
Don't succeed to meet
The day.
Any travelers
Don't reach
their destination.
Some fighters
Offer themselves
To win,
But they don't enjoy
This victory's result.
In this bit of history
There's life anyway.
Life regenerates
Again and again.
Step by step
Something happens
And this changes you,
This marks your path.
That night
Was a step of this kind
For me.
Night, life, path met
And they
Got to an agreement.

XL.

May you

May you
>Be lucky
May you
>Have a broad way
>Where you walk
May you
>Feel always love
>In and around you
May you
>See the sons
>Of your sons
May
>The blessings of God
>Smile on you
All your life long.

Impaginato per conto di Officina della Sibilla
nel mese di agosto dell'anno 2016

www.officinadellasibilla.it

Finito di stampare nel mese di Settembre 2016
per conto di Youcanprint *Self-Publishing*